Love's Glory

RE-CREATIONS OF RUMI

To the Unity
Library

In Love
Ruth[?]
November '99

Love's Glory

RE-CREATIONS OF RUMI

Andrew Harvey

Balthazar Books
San Francisco, California

North Atlantic Books
Berkeley, California

Love's Glory: Re-creations of Rumi

Published by Balthazar Books and North Atlantic Books

Balthazar Books
3739 Balboa Street, Box 182
San Francisco, California 94121

North Atlantic Books
P.O. Box 12327
Berkeley, California 94712

Cover photograph © Eryk Hanut
Cover and book design by Paula Morrison
Printed in the United States of America

Love's Glory: Re-creations of Rumi is sponsored in part by the Society for the Study of Native Arts and Sciences, a nonprofit educational corporation whose goals are to develop an educational and crosscultural perspective linking various scientific, social, and artistic fields; to nurture a holistic view of the arts, sciences, humanities, and healing; and to publish and distribute literature on the relationship of mind, body, and nature.

1/00

Library of Congress Cataloging-in-Publication Data
Harvey, Andrew, 1952–
    Love's glory : re-creations of Rumi / [adapted by] Andrew Harvey.
      p. cm.
    "The vast majority of the poems are taken from Rumi's Rubaiyat."
—CIP pref.
    ISBN 1-55643-225-9 (pbk.)
    1. Sufi poetry, English.   2. Mysticism—Poetry.   I. Jalāl al-Dīn
Rūmī, Maulana, 1207–1273. Rubā Iyāt. English. Selections. 1996.
PR6058.A6986L68   1996
821'.914—dc20   96–12370
                                                            CIP

1   2   3   4   5   6   7   8   9 / 00   99   98   97   96

V

For Leila Hadley Luce,
who knows Love's Glory

Introduction

These short poems by Jalal-ud-Din Rumi, humanity's most passionate and exalted mystic poet, are telegrams from Supreme Consciousness, sharp, dazzling, electric messages directly from Rumi's Awakened Heart to our own, word-mirrors held up to us by Love itself so we can glimpse our own real face.

No one has left us a richer, wilder, or more lucid witness to the glory of Divine Love than Rumi; his testimony to Love's immensity and to the ordeals and revelations of its unfolding in the soul is one of humanity's indispensable documents. Rumi reminds us all, whoever we are and on whatever path we find ourselves, of the inherent magnificence of the Heart and of the mystery and majesty of that Identity we all share as children of the Sun and potential lovers of the Beloved.

In the vast, terrifying, worldwide crisis we find ourselves in, such testimony to the essential wonder and value of life is essential to our survival. How will we find the courage, passion, and soul-force to unite and work to preserve the planet if we do not know who—

and where—we really are? What else can give us the strength and inspiration we need to bear whatever hardships and sacrifices are ahead but a vision of our real divine nature, and of the real divine nature of human life and the world? Rumi's vision of the soul and of the glory of the human enterprise is one of the grandest and bravest we have ever been given. From the Light that he is and lives in, beyond space and time, Rumi is radiating to a darkening world the light of his infinite love and hope, urging us all onward, whatever our belief and unbelief, into the miracle of our authentic divine truth and the feast of the divine life on earth. On whether we listen to him—and those visionaries like him—and on whether we act on what we hear and learn—depends the future.

This collection of 108 poems is my attempt to pass on, in as concentrated a form as possible, the invigoration, instruction, and fierce encouragement that I have received from Rumi over many years of trying to follow his Way of Passion. I have arranged them as a dance around crucial mystical themes: nondual bliss, ordeal, ecstatic recognition, revelation, and gratitude. The vast majority of the poems are taken from Rumi's *Rubaiyat,* a collection of 2,000 quatrains; a very few are adapted from couplets from the *Odes* or from particularly pregnant and illuminating phrases from the *Discourses*. I have worked from literal versions and from a plethora of translations in different languages and, most especially, from those in French by Eva de Vitray-Meyerovitch.

May the Lover in all of us be awakened by these poems, and may we all, awoken in Love's Glory, act in Love's Name to transform conditions on earth and so save ourselves—and our world—from catastrophe.

Andrew Harvey
January, 1996
San Francisco

Love's Glory

RE-CREATIONS OF RUMI

You need money, the love of friends,
You need your health, you need laughter.
Most of all you need what only He gives:
The living presence of Divine Grace.

Green Fire is the Sign of the New Body
My love and yours engenders in the bed of dawn.
Green fire licks all pride from the skull
Soaks each trembling cell with heaven.

"Speak of Love's Glory? How do you dare?"
I gave my mouth to God to do with what He
    wanted.
For years, He buried it at the bottom of His sea
Today He raises it, rimmed with living pearls.

You can never see Him if you don't see you *are* Him.
Could the waterdrop ever reach the Sea
If it didn't know the Sea is boiling inside it?
"Don't speak any more," He said, "honor My
Mystery!"

It is a burning of the heart I want
It is this burning I want more than anything
It is this burning in the core of the heart
That calls God secretly in the night.

They prattle of "balance," of "moderation," of
    "decorum."
I wrote on one of their doors in secret:
"You think you know, you died long ago;
  You think you see? Reason ate your eyes."

Long ago, I left "heaven" and "earth"
Slipped out of time and ran beyond the timeless.
"Where are you then?" they ask; what can I say?
One look from my Lover, and I'm struck dumb.

I heard Your coming on the wind
I heard the nightingale repeat Your name
I saw a strange image on the door of my heart
They are talking about it softly on Your roof.

Andrew Harvey

"Run to the window," You said in the dream, and I ran.
 A sea vaster than the world reared its gorgeous head
    like a snake
 A brilliant pure blue Sea vaster than any horizon—
 And from its growling storm-core, as it reared,
    blazed You.

Who could have survived that Blazing from the Sea?
Your dogs of terror tore apart what little remained
I awoke to find myself in millions of pieces
Each of them radiant with me-and-You.

When I am the Sea
Each atom flames out of me.
I blaze! Each moment is
This one total moment.

Without the fire of Your love, I'd never drink this
    water
Without your Face's features, I'd never see this Vision
In Your water, pouring through me like pure wine,
I groan and turn like a millwheel.

What have I to win or lose? I am Being,
Love's calmest glory; silence of eons
Sustaining, enduring, feeding Its own Creation
You, me, the words and silences between us.

The soul soars towards the world of the King
She'll win there a heart beyond "how" or "why"
And the mystery that was hidden only yesterday
Will be revealed beyond the thousand veils.

If you want to discover Eternal Life
And live in the radiant desert of Detachment
Advance bravely on the Path, fearing no pain or loss,
Take each step authentically, risking your whole being.

Never think it is time that killed me
I was killed by the Source of the Water of Life.
If an enemy killed you, that would be terrible but
    normal;
I was killed by the soul of my soul.

No one knows who I am, no one can find me,
No one can hurt me, no one can destroy me.
O Beloved! You have lifted me clear of "me"
Fate's arrows rain on an old rag doll.

Allow yourself to break, so you can know
    My Certainty
Live My Fragility, so you can come into
    My Strength
My Majesty is eternal, yet trembles in each flower
My Power is deathless, yet weeps at each death.

Without You in me how could I bear one moment
This grief of living without You?
And these tears—aren't they You rising in me
To flood me ruthlessly towards Your hidden arms?

The universe contemplates nothing but Your Face
Souls when they see You weep and tear off their skins
To the eyes of those whom passion has made wise
Your madness is the Diamond, the Fountain of
    Paradise.

The stone doesn't have to become a rose to have all
   gardens in it
Things don't have to shift shape to be Infinity's
   mirrors ...
This world, You said, is madder than the maddest
   madman's dreams
Doors fly open in each atom: You stand laughing in
   them all.

In this world of splitting mirrors, what looks out
Or looks in, looks in a thousand zig-zag ways—
Look at these eyes now, look at how they look—
Who is this Sun-Man leaping out in laughter?

How can I be all things and nothing and not be mad?
And yet it's clear this ladybird in the grass
Proclaims *"I am"* with my most secret voice
And wind in its frail marvelous wings writes Your
  name.

I thought I had exhausted terror, being trampled
To become Your dust, finer and finer ...
Then the night came when You whispered "I am you"
And vanished, leaving me everywhere nowhere.

Know now, at once, all atoms everywhere in all worlds
Are fire-dancing out of their mind for love of Him
This crazy ecstatic dancing is the One Reality
Storm after storm of Passion on a Bed of Peace.

I laugh with my whole body, like the rose,
And not with my lips only.
I have thrown myself over my head
To stand naked with the King of Spring.

Despair of all things, of all you have known of God
Fall through death after death into the Lap of
    Darkness ...
I will wait for you there, where you no longer know
    Me.
I will wait for you there, where you are no longer
    yourself.

Tonight the knowers of the mysteries are drunk
Seated in ecstasy behind the veil with the Friend.
Marvelous strange existence! Keep away from our
    door!
Strangers tonight belong to a different world.

Normal divinity keeps me still on my chair
Lord of all worlds; no need to go anywhere.
The heart is "Light upon Light." And you, my Heart,
Beat out afresh every living Light-moment.

The Burning Bush has come; it must put us to the test
We wanted Revelation and now we must burn
You said "yes" at the beginning, why do you shrink
    now?
Become a salamander; make a house of fire.

Don't bow your head to the ground
Raise it ecstatically and become
Like the spring-awoken peach tree
All freshness, all smile.

From the first moment I knew You through love
How many hidden games we've played!
Come closer, Drunken One, to the tent of my heart
I've emptied it of everything for You, for You.

Yesterday my whole being begged Him in secret:
"Don't go on keeping the Secret secret!"
Gently, so gently, He whispered in me:
"It can be known and seen, but never spoken."

Ruin has a secret name not even Splendor knows
Death a laughter even seraphim have never heard
Time's bloody fingers work tapestries of Eternal Grace
You want to see their Order? Go mad with love.

I know at last I know nothing; Ignorance
On such a scale, dazzles and frees my soul
Child-wonder becomes my daily bread
Broken for me each passing moment.

In the mirror of My Fire see your own desire

See how My eyes flame out with your own power

Sparks of My Splendor fell on you and fed you My
Strength

Who bears My Horror in you? I Myself.

Love made a ruin of my heart
The Sun of Suns came and shone
It was He, the King, who prayed for me
And He who granted His own prayer.

Water in cup or stream is shaken by secret hands
Have you never seen Light trembling on a wall?
Nature is Him, my friend, One Dance, One Body
Flashing out each moment with His Miracle.

I cannot ruin the Mystery
I cannot reveal what I know perfectly—
In the most secret core of me, something blazes joy
I can never put a finger on it....

Not one (I still exist to say this), and yet not two
A Sea of Light Is, of which we are both waves ...
"No," he smiled, "You and I are both wave and
    sea...."
"How can I understand?" "You can't," he said, "But
    you can love."

There's another language beyond language
Another heaven beyond heaven and hell
Our hearts live by another heart
What we are shines from a placeless place.

Knowing you know and can know nothing opens
The small Light-window between your heart and His
And keeps it wide open: messages come and go
    endlessly
From Him to you, from you to Him, from
    Him-in-you to you-in-Him.

I hunger for those dust storms that whirl from our
   heaven

I've known so much Apocalypse, nothing terrifies
   me now

My soul smiles and laughs: behind the mirror of
   Your butchery

She sees your Face-in-Love as you savage and kill.

Your anger opened for me the Gates of Heaven
The despair Your fury flung me in
Pried apart the Flame-Door to the Garden
I ran in and broke into Myself.

I unlock the Door from inside to myself
Step from room to room leading myself
Come to myself in myself in our Bed of Fire
Hear You astoundedly call Yourself by my name.

What can a Lover do, if he's not ruined by You?
How can nights blaze if they don't burn in Your house?
Don't find me absurd if I kiss the rings of Your curls
What can a madman do but bite at his chains?

"Faith" and "Proof" and "Certainty"
   All eye me with savage jealousy.
   My heart has put on His belt of Suns,
   My body turned to musk in His Sea.

When in my heart the lightning of love arises
I know it is flashing and rearing in His heart also.
And when in ecstasy I can say only His Name
I know it is His Passion that erupts from me.

The man who isn't crazy for You is a blasphemer
The one who isn't shattered by You has no soul
I can't even consider Universal Reason rational
If I don't see it mad and dishonored by passion.

I tear up the roots of agony or cure
I tear up the roots of tyranny or slavery ...
Did you see how passionately I repented?
I tear up the roots of repentance, and dance.

Be the Lover of God day and night
You'll live forever beyond day or night.
See what he has given and laugh for joy:
Cupbearer, wine, cup—all are eternal.

Don't talk to me of "heaven," heaven's for believers,
Long ago I abandoned believing for knowing.
I don't need any heaven when I have You here
Here with You is the only heaven I need.

I'm drunk, I know, but on His Face
Drowned, yes, but in His wine-river …
It's His sugar, His flower garden, that have fed me
I'm speaking here, but with His voice.

Like Christ, You fly over
Dry and humid nature
Split the abyss, open the roads,
Become their final direction.

On the roof, under His moon and exploding stars,
Lucidity's a fool, a fraud, a liar—
The Mystery of Majesty is ringed by darkness
Only the stunned and bewildered ever glimpse the
    Throne.

They called me "traitor": I slept in Your arms
They said I was "evil": I drank from Your lips
They said I knew nothing; You fed me Your sugar
They said I'd be forgotten; You said "Live forever!"

They say they love, and make such dainty distinctions
If they'd seen the Fire, could they name it flame by
    flame?
One moment of madness, their soul would be a ruin
I pray for them all: Ruin them before they die.

The soul, my friend, became a stranger
Reason, my doctor, became mad
Kings have hidden treasures in ruins
Our ruin is a ruin because of treasure.

Know you know nothing always, my heart, so His
    Glory
Can go on writing Wonder on your ever-fresh snow
Unknow them at once, the Secrets will all flower
Let awe dumb you, the Hidden Names unveil.

In dazzled drunk amazement, love's most
     transforming power
The world's illusion peels away only for You ...
The Beloved's virgin soul keeps the King a child
Now Your heart is child too, His Miracle can appear.

If your every single breath became a prayer
You'd see atoms as angels and hear in each wind
The whirr of Love's wings, and feel in each moment
The Beloved pulling you into His heart.

I slashed the veils of Mind until I stumbled on
    Mystery
And knew as I stood there aghast at its dark Fire
That one step forward and I'd forever be undone—
You took that step in me, the two worlds became
    One.

Your body is more subtle than soul or heart
There's a long Path between sugar and Your lips
How long the sun and moon have been turning
Day and night, just to spend one night with You!

One hope, and one hope only: Your Love.
One strength, and one strength only: Your Love.
Until each cell cries out and ceaselessly invokes You
The world reels only from illusion to illusion.

"Be my Nothing," You said, "and my Secret will flash
   out...."

Around Your Sun of Nothing worlds whirl in bliss
   forever

When You cry out in me I am everything I am
   nothing

All men in me in You witness One Identity, One
   Love.

Hand in hand with the Moon
Hand in hand with the Sun
Shall I call myself man or woman?
O Lover, you have no sex, no name.

Eternity waits behind the transparent door
Of each moment. Love the Beloved, and that door
Swings open: Eternity enters, pouring the wine
No one who drinks can ever recover from.

Weeping over the Beloved's beauty like a lover
Naming to the heart each created thing
Baptizing each thing in the heart's tears
Tears of searing, tears of praise.

A drunken nightingale sings for me in each moment,
In the wind I hear our dance music always playing.
Streams run and leap, I see Your Image sparkling;
In all the spring flowers, smell only You.

In this mad world, kings wander desperate as slaves
Rulers of the universe die begging a glass of water . . .
"Announce My Identity," You said to everyone who
    lives,
"I'm tired of being hidden, I want My Face to rule!"

Only hosanna is real, only Adoration is wise
The Fire in the heart awakens to the Fire outside
Burning all veils so Fire meets Fire in the water-
    mirror
Lover, Beloved, now are only words.

This mystery: the sea of the worlds suddenly parts
To reveal everywhere Your burning desert.
Step onto that sand, and all feet turn to ash
Run forward, even prophets become smoke.

What veil could remain between You and me?
The only veil was me, and You burned me away
Beloved, in my ash, You have written Your name
All things now are madmen dancing in our fire.

My Beloved is mine like the air I breathe
The earth I walk on is Him, and so are my feet
I thought He was Being; He smiled, and Being
    vanished
Reappeared as Non-Being, ablaze with Him.

Come, come, for today
I'm sprung of the universe
Come, come, today I became
Invisible to myself

If for one evening, my Beauty, you do not sleep
The treasure of eternity will flash out secretly
The Sun of the invisible will warm you all night
Mystery lead you through room after room of
  Revelation.

No one can walk on water, they say,
Or climb up Sinai without feet.
My heart has run on water all day
And will pray on Sinai all night.

Be alive, be alive in Love
Dead men can do nothing.
Who is alive in this world of ghosts?
He whom Love keeps birthing.

Death breaks the cage, but doesn't wound the bird
What can death do to the feathers of the phoenix?
Be silent at last! You've been talking a long time ...
Let silence transform your mind to gaze.

Between Me and you no barriers
Heart-to-heart talk, Eye-to-eye
On the pillow
Of Eternity.

The Holy Balance You are only the mad discover;
The clearest diamond is at the bottom of the ash.
I brought You my Being, You pushed it into Your
  Fire
It blazed through madness into Rigor.

Fools believe that knowing brings them power
Such power-knowing is just another hollow
The only real knowing is Loving, for when
Mystery begins, only Love can follow.

Limitless Void!
Splendor into which all forms vanish!
You have appeared in my forehead
Like my own diamond.

No words between us now
Although I seem to speak
This is only Your Love
Brimming over my cup.

The extreme helplessness of Love
Is exactly like dying—
Beyond any control,
An agony of birth.

No one has ever heard me but Myself
No one has ever loved me but Myself
No one has ever denied me but Myself
No one has ever seen me but Myself

Love Him with your whole heart and mind and soul
So He can infuse your soul with a new soul
Its Eye in you will burn through all veils
See the whole cosmos your own Fire-breath.

Real lovers who live in the House of Love
Are moths seared with the torch of His Face
Hurry there, my heart! He wants to blaze out in you
Unveil His sweet fire-garden after His Terror.

Beyond this flame-desert, other, even wilder deserts,
And then beyond them, kingdoms, kingdoms
    without end.
You want to "arrive"? You know so little yet!
Love's wine is endless; go on pouring it forever.

Run now, it is time, into the House of Wine
That's where in the end all Lovers live.
Run there now, enter, and seize the cup
Madness holds out to you with laughing hands.

Nurse of my spirit in its hour of ordeal!

Treasure of my heart in the agony of its need!

What imagination could not shape and knowledge
   not know

Has shone from You slowly to my astounded soul.

Mine of Beauty and Miracle, who owns You?
How can I pick You, Lightning-Flower?
For all its tongues, the lily could not tell me.
"Go away!" it said. "All I can do is praise."

Be quiet and tear the thorn of Being from your heart
Uncover in silence your soul's own rose garden.
He is the sun hidden in this cloud of words
Be still: let Him turn the whole sky to fire.

The whole of time today is mine
The wheel of Heaven reels with me
In the whirlwind of the Country of Nowhere
I receive the orders of the King.

What I imagined desert turned out to be Sea

Annihilation in one ecstasy revealed itself Origin

I composed bitter blasphemies but spoke words of
    pure love

I plotted to destroy You, but became You instead.

O Wine of Love, Your passion makes justice perfect
One cup of You, a thousand slaves soar free
I cried Your Name of Freedom and the sky exploded,
Raining Heaven on earth.

One Flash of Your Cup, and the next moment
I'm pouring wine for prostitutes and madmen.
One glimpse of Your Lightning-Crown,
I'm dancing headless.

I arrive in me in each face, each sound, each event.
Who could ever explain this crazy game we play?
We are not one, and not two, and we are
What no words will ever be able to say.

My Balance rises like a phoenix from the ash of
    extremes
No one can ever live it who has not burnt away.
My Peace is only poured for the one prepared
To drown all peace in final passion.

When I live in Action, I can seem to do nothing
The two worlds will be turning because of me.
When I live in Action, I can be working feverishly
My heart holds all worlds in its calm eternity.

I'm old, you say? I've never been younger

I've unwound back to before I was born.

Reality leaps from my womb, I'm the juice in each
    vine,

The Light-wine all things are wet with deep down.

When will grief go and live among the slaves of the
     King
In the Palace where all things are Feast and Mirror?
There is something more vast than joy that exists—
I felt it once, my whole being became soul.

I drank the philter of Your passion
O Water of Life—I drank, and became You.
Death came, and smelled Your fragrance all over me
Death himself grew drunk, and forgot to kill.

I looked for a soul: it was in a sea of coral
Hidden under the foam of a secret ocean.
In the night of my heart, by a narrow path,
I traveled on and on and came to Your desert.

Each humiliation I bless, each loss, each agony
Only death after death could have brought me
To this bare sun-dazzled desert where
You gush up in everything.

No end to the journey, no end, no end ever . . .
How can the Heart-in-Love ever stop opening?
"If you love Me," He said, "you won't just die once.
In every moment you'll die into Me, to be reborn."

A perfect love, a splendor beyond praise
A heart full of words, a silent mouth—
How can so strange a state of being be?
I am thirsty: pure water streams through me.

When I die, burn me
The smoke from this body
Will write in the air
His name, His name.

Acknowledgments

My deepest thanks to:

Marianne Dresser, fellow Rumi lover and the most helpful, honest, and encouraging of editors.

Paula Morrison, for her openness and beautiful design.

Lisa and John Hunt, for the truth of their love.

Eryk Hanut, my beloved husband, for his cover photograph, his indispensable help in the final selection of the poems, and his wild love.

Marlene, for being who she is.

Karen Kelledjian, whose friendship illumines my world.

Balthazar, Gino, Cookie, Loopy, Debbie, and Ana, for the unfailing, magical tenderness of their presence in Eryk's and my life.